Home With Mom and Dad

S0-EGS-955

by Mickey Daronco and Diane Ohanesian

I am at home
with Mom and Dad.
I hope we will have fun
at home.

I can tell Dad a joke.
Will Dad get the joke?

We can all play
with a big rope.
We will have fun
with the big rope.

Dad can poke my small nose.
Will I poke
his big nose back?

Dad can get the big hose.
Will I get the big hose
with Dad?

I can sit and pose.
I hope Mom and Dad
will pose for me.

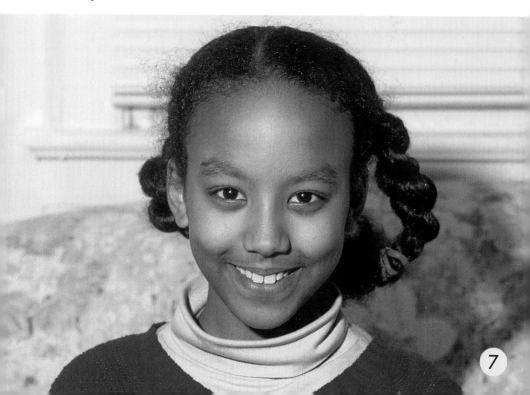

7

Dad can get a big red rose.

It is a rose for Mom.

I can get a big, big red rose.

It is a rose for Mom, too.